Thermal Underwear

A Comedy

Andrew Davies

Samuel French – London
New York – Sydney – Toronto – Hollywood

Copyright © 1987 by Andrew Davies
All Rights Reserved

THERMAL UNDERWEAR is fully protected under the copyright laws of the British Commonwealth, including Canada, the United States of America, and all other countries of the Copyright Union. All rights, including professional and amateur stage productions, recitation, lecturing, public reading, motion picture, radio broadcasting, television and the rights of translation into foreign languages are strictly reserved.

ISBN 978-0-573-12273-6

www.samuelfrench.co.uk
www.samuelfrench.com

For Amateur Production Enquiries

United Kingdom and World excluding North America

plays@SamuelFrench-London.co.uk

020 7255 4302/01

Each title is subject to availability from Samuel French, depending upon country of performance.

CAUTION: Professional and amateur producers are hereby warned that *THERMAL UNDERWEAR* is subject to a licensing fee. Publication of this play does not imply availability for performance. Both amateurs and professionals considering a production are strongly advised to apply to the appropriate agent before starting rehearsals, advertising, or booking a theatre. A licensing fee must be paid whether the title is presented for charity or gain and whether or not admission is charged.

The professional rights in this play are controlled by The Agency (London) Ltd, 24 Pottery Lane, Holland Park, London W11 4LZ.

No one shall make any changes in this title for the purpose of production. No part of this book may be reproduced, stored in a retrieval system, or transmitted in any form, by any means, now known or yet to be invented, including mechanical, electronic, photocopying, recording, videotaping, or otherwise, without the prior written permission of the publisher. No one shall upload this title, or part of this title, to any social media websites.

The right of Andrew Davies to be identified as author of this work has been asserted in accordance with Section 77 of the Copyright, Designs and Patents Act 1988.

THERMAL UNDERWEAR

First performed at the Tri-Ads Theatre Festival, Library Theatre, Solihull, in September, 1986, by the Henley-in-Arden Drama Society with the following cast:

Elaine	Kay Tandy
Bob	Roy Jones
Mum	Beryl Butler
Dad	Alan Butler
Shirley	Fiona Sutherland-Jones
Gareth	Philip Dale

Directed by John Alcock
Designer Barbara Alcock
Stage Manager John Shuttleworth

THERMAL UNDERWEAR

Bob's and Elaine's living-room. Sunday lunchtime

There is a door to the kitchen and another door leading to the rest of the house. Upstage there is a hi-fi cabinet with a phone and a table with a tray of drinks. On the coffee-table in front of the sofa is a bulky parcel in wrapping paper

As the CURTAIN *rises the introduction music fades and we hear Elaine singing upstairs*

Elaine (*singing, off*) "Every step you take, Every move you make..."

The loose board on the landing emits its sound; a sort of mournful, long quack

(*Speaking, off*) And *you* can shut up too!

Elaine comes in briskly and makes for the phone. She is dressed in a slip. She is in her mid-thirties. Her energy, her appetite, are apparent in everything she says and does. She sits on a stool and dials. Her free hand comes up to stroke herself. She is expecting to get Mick on the phone but she gets Shirley. She bangs the phone down

Damn. (*Her fingers go into her mouth as she thinks furiously. Then she dials again*) Hello Shirley, Elaine.... What?... No, yes, yes, it was. Suddenly went dead on me. Like one or two other things round here, if you ... no, the rabbit's fine, he's game for anything, he chewed up Liddie's Sony Walkperson the day before yesterday.... I wasn't talking about rabbits, Shirley. ... Mm. Well, who else?... Actually I think he's been trying to tap it or something. Keep getting all these funny little tweaks and flutters.... The *phone*, Shirley.... Well, I don't know. It gives him an interest. Quite flattering, in a way. Well, you are coming, aren't you? Bob's just gone round to fetch them. ... Well, of *course* we want you here. *They* want you to be here. Mick's got a bit of life about him, that's what Mum always says, trust Mick to put the cat among the pigeons, whatever she thought she meant by that, but she's right. And you, of course. ... What d'you mean, he's got one of his things? ... Just suddenly came up? ... But he will be here, won't he, he knows we're counting on both of you. ... Well, I do hope so, Shirley. What *sort* of thing has he got? ... (*Delighted*) Shirley, that's rude. Well, look, you just bundle him into the car and get him round, Shirley, got to dash now, I'm practically naked here, see you, Shirley, bye. (*She puts the phone down*)

There is the sound of a car stopping outside

Oh, God.

She makes for the door fast, as we hear car doors slam and the front door open off. She stops just before she goes out

Mick Crawford if you don't show up today I'll kill you.

Elaine goes out as Bob brings in Elaine's parents. Mrs Hudd (referred to hereafter as Mum) is a lively old lady who sees the funny side of things and looks on the bright side of life. Dad, Mr Hudd, is not in good shape. He can walk about all right, but he doesn't seem to pay attention to what's going on. He has that look of having been dressed by somebody else

Bob (*rather frantically stripping their coats off*) Right, then, here we are, that's it, warm enough for you in here I hope, there we are, you just er, and I'll just take these in the ... (*He stops just before disappearing with the coats. With some savagery*) Elaine!

Bob goes

Elaine (*off*) I know!

Mum and Dad sit on the sofa. Dad stares straight ahead

Mum Well, this is very nice. Arty Farty gave a party, but nobody came! (*She laughs*) Oh dear, I haven't thought of that in years!

She gives Dad a poke. He reacts slightly but irritably

Thermal Underwear

Where was Moses when the lights went out?

She digs him again, again he reacts

Talk to yourself.

The mournful quack of the loose board upstairs

Dad They haven't fixed that board yet.
Mum (*calling to Bob*) Girls not here, Bob?

The sound of the board again

Dad Grates on me.

Bob comes back

Bob Elaine! (*As before*) Sorry, what was that?
Dad I've got a good mind to go up there and give it a few whacks.
Bob What?
Mum (*to Dad*) Shut up, you. (*To Bob*) The girls. Asking about the girls. Are they not here, then?
Bob No, unfortunately, they're not; they wanted to be here, they said, but not enough to actually make the effort, apparently; and as you know I have absolutely no influence on their behaviour, otherwise I should of course have insisted, but there you are, the excuses are a charity fun run in Sarah's case, and Tai-Kwan-Do Green Belt Trials in Liddie's. And if you think that sounds improbably healthy and virtuous, you may well be right, for all I know they may be indulging in unspeakable rites with pot-bellied thirty-five year old motorcycle freaks, or simply putting in a few hours with the local glue-sniffers on the common. Elaine!
Mum (*amused by this*) Oh dear, oh dear, hear that, Dad? He says the girls won't be here, they've gone glue-sniffing! Well, you're only young once, aren't you?
Bob Yes, that is a point of view one often hears, and I suppose one could say that a period of say twenty-five years of emotional immaturity and financial dependence *only happens once*, but it does take rather a long time to happen, unlike other things that *only happen once*, such as, shall we say, one's grandparents' Ruby Wedding Anniversary party, which only takes a couple of hours out of a whole bloody lifetime, d'you see, and one might have thought that Sarah and Liddie could have spared a couple

of hours out of the relentless round of self-indulgence known as Being Young to put a bloody frock on and sit round getting bored out their skulls with the rest of us, if you follow my drift.

Mum *laughing*) Oh, he's a bobby-dazzler, isn't he, Dad? I've always said, always, I don't care what they say about our Elaine's Bob, that man is a brilliant conversationalist.

Bob Thank you very much indeed.

Mum Talk about wit flying about, mind you you can't believe a word he says, but you have to laugh, don't you?

Bob (*more to himself as he goes to the door leading upstiars*) No, I don't actually *quite* grasp why you have to do that ... Elaine!

Elaine (*off*) What?

Bob I was just wondering if you'd realized, darling, that your parents have been sitting down here waiting for you for the past ten minutes?

Elaine (*off*) Oh darling, have they really? Well do you want me to come straight down stark naked, or d'you think you could possibly hang on two minutes while I get *dressed*?

Bob (*with grave courtesy*) Elaine's just getting dressed, she should be down in an hour or two.

Mum Down in an hour or two, hear that, Dad, down in an hour or two, not far off that with our Elaine, eh, will of her own, that one.

The board creaks

Dad You want to get that board fixed.

Bob Perhaps I could offer you a drink?

Dad Really grates on me that.

Mum No, Bob, don't you worry about us, we'll wait till everyone else comes.

Dad Got a good mind to give it a few whacks myself. Yes. I'll have a drink.

Mum No you won't, no he won't, take no notice of him Bob, we'll wait for everyone else, we know how to enjoy ourselves without alcohol, don't we Dad?

Bob Do you really, that's—that's quite an accomplishment these days ... (*Getting a bit vague as he's just noticed Elaine's handbag which she's left downstairs*) Would you excuse me one second? (*He grabs the handbag and starts rooting about in it*)

Mum Who else is coming then, Bob?

Thermal Underwear

Bob Oh, you know . . . just family. Well, more or less family. Well, Gareth and Veronica and Shirley and Mick, in point of fact. Just the usual scintillating gang. Can't *quite* see why we always have to have them, but it seems we do. (*He pulls out Elaine's diary and starts leafing through it*) Hmm. (*He puts it back and unzips another compartment*)

Mum Well Gareth and Veronica *are* family.

Bob And Shirley and Mick are such bloody awful people they might just as well be family, yes. I sometimes catch myself thinking we must in some way *be* blood relatives, otherwise why would we know them, the notion that we must at some point have chosen them as friends seems too bizarre to contemplate.

Mum Oh, I like that Mick, he's got a bit of life about him, hasn't he, Dad? Oh, dear. That inflatable banana. Remember that banana, Dad?

No reaction from Dad

Have you lost something, Bob?

Bob (*a bitter laugh*) Ha!

Mum There was a thing in our paper about that. Wasn't there, Dad? In the *A to Z of the Darker Side of Love*. R, it was. Rooting about in ladies handbags. "These pathetic men", it said, well I can't remember how it went, I couldn't be doing with it, and neither could Dad, could you, Dad? Not much he can be doing with, still, there you are, well, well, well.

Bob (*in suppressed rage; still rooting*) I don't root about in ladies' handbags, Mother-in-law, I only root about in my wife's handbag.

Mum Well, I think that's very nice, Bob.

Elaine (*off, from above*) Ready!

The board quacks again. Dad looks up sharply and opens his mouth

Mum Don't you dare!

He shuts it. Bob replaces the stuff in the handbag and closes it

Dad Want to get that board fixed.

Elaine comes in wearing a dress and high heels. She looks quite sexy. She is dressed for Mick

Elaine (*going straight to them*) Hello, Mummy. (*She kisses her*)

Daddy. (*She kisses him*) Don't you look smart. And sorry. He would go over early, he knew I wasn't ready. All his fault.
Bob Naturally.
Elaine Well. Look at you. Forty years together and still going strong!
Mum (*laughing*) Doesn't bear thinking about, does it?
Bob No, it doesn't.
Elaine Bob.
Bob (*recovering*) I do beg your pardon. I am genuinely very impressed. Forty years of happy marriage to the same person seems to me a quite astonishing achievement. Barely credible. But ... here you are.
Mum Oh, well, you know yourselves, it's easy as pie when you've got into the swing of it, Bob!
Bob (*thoughtfully*) Is it? Is it? D'you know, I don't believe I *have* got ...
Dad First thirty-nine years are the worst.
Mum (*laughing*) There he goes! You'd think he was miles away, but he's not, are you, Dad? Sharp as a tack!

She nudges him. He reacts irritably

Bob I was wondering actually if you could give me a bit of advice.

The doorbell rings

Elaine Oh, that'll be Mick and Shirley, I'll get it.

Elaine goes

Mum What about, Bob?
Bob Oh ... marriage. Life. How to ... get through them. Thought you might have a few hints.
Dad Give you a hint about that board upstairs.
Bob No, that wasn't quite what I ...

Shirley comes in followed by Elaine

Shirley Well here I am at last then, Gareth and Veronica not here yet, thought I'd be last, thought I wouldn't get here at all, we've had such a crisis with the rats, hello Mrs Hudd, Mr Hudd, don't you look wonderful, forty years, well that's a real example to us all! Hello Bob, darling.
Bob (*tonelessly*) Hello Shirley.

Shirley He's a sexy beast, isn't he? In his little jumper.
Mum Got rats, then, have you, Shirley, that's a bit of a trial. Very persistent, rats are.
Elaine In the *lab*, Mother, you *know* that, she works in a lab, don't you, Shirley, they're laboratory rats, and you've heard all about them, and they're not very interesting, are they, Shirley?
Shirley Yes, they are.
Elaine What have you done with Mick?
Shirley I haven't done anything with him, Elaine. He had to pop up the road. So I came on ahead. You know what he's like, popping up the road. I thought I'll come on ahead. Well you know what he's like. "I've got to pop up the road," he says, "got something on, it won't take long."
Elaine Well, I hope it doesn't, Shirley.
Shirley Well, it doesn't usually. But you know what he's like, when he's got something on. No stopping him.
Elaine Yes, I know. I'm the same myself.
Shirley Well, there you are then.

Pause. During the pause Mum beams around amiably and hums audibly, quite unaware of any tension in the atmosphere

Elaine What road has he popped up, Shirley?

Pause

Shirley I don't know, Elaine, he didn't say. Not this one, though, clearly.
Elaine No. But he does hope to get along later.
Shirley Oh, yes, I think so, Elaine. He doesn't usually take long, well you know that.
Mum Well I hope he does, Shirley, wouldn't be the same without Mick, would it? He's got a bit of life about him, he knows how to put the cat among the pigeons!
Elaine (*in a state of some emotional turmoil*) Well, I've got some bits and bobs to see to in the kitchen.

Elaine turns and goes out to the kitchen

Shirley I'll just go up to your bathroom, Elaine, ours is still full of newts as you can well imagine, give you a hand when I get down. (*To Bob, as she goes to the door leading upstairs*) Cheer up, Tiger.

Shirley goes

Mum Full of *newts*?
Bob What it was, the thing I wanted your advice about ... we're going through a bit of a difficult patch, Elaine and I ... daresay you might have noticed.
Mum Oh, dear, that's a shame, isn't it, Dad?

The board quacks upstairs. Dad looks up. The pauses marked * during the following are not "emotional stress" pauses but "searching for the right word" pauses

Bob And I thought, from your long experience ... you see the thing is, she's being unfaithful to me, she's having an affair with someone, she seems to be (*pause**) in the grip of uncontrollable lust for another man ... I hope this isn't embarrassing for you?
Mum No, no, Bob, all friends here, well if you can't talk to your own mother and father-in-law who can you talk to, you go on, pet. Hear that about our Elaine, Dad?

No reaction

You go on, love, he's dead to the world, this one.
Bob Well, this sort of thing (*pause**) a lot of people seem to take it in their stride, but somehow that doesn't seem to be an option for me, I'm (*pause**) I'm consumed with jealousy.
Mum Oh, dear, that's a shame, isn't it, Dad?
Bob I, er, I begged her to stop, but, well, she sort of laughed in my face and told me to mind my own business.
Mum (*laughing merrily*) Well, that's our Elaine for you! Gareth, now, butter wouldn't melt in his mouth, but she was always the sparky one. "Where you been?" "Out playing." "Who with?" "None of your business." Oh, she was always a cheeky monkey. Couldn't do a thing with her.
Bob Yes, quite. Anyway, recently, I've found my thoughts revolving around what you might call terminal violence.
Mum (*politely*) Oh, yes?
Bob Yes, I thought of sort of strangling her and then blowing my brains out, sort of thing.
Mum (*laughing merrily*) Oh, dear, the things you young ones come out with, hear that Dad, never a dull moment here!

Bob Well that's as far as my thinking has got at the moment, I was wondering whether you had any comments.
Mum Oh, well, Bob, I'll have to put my thinking cap on, won't I?
Bob I'd be enormously grateful for your input.
Mum Mm. Well now, don't you think that sort of thing just withers away with time, Bob? I mean, that's what we've found, haven't we, Dad, and weighing up the one against the other it's a blessing on the whole. I mean, she can't be all that far off the change, can she, our Elaine, and that'll slow her up a bit, won't it?
Bob She's thirty-*five*, Mother.
Mum And then you've got a lovely home and two lovely girls, and you've both got your health ... and well, love, we've always said, say what you like about Bob, he's got a head on him. Brains in there he hasn't even used yet.

Bob looks puzzled for a moment

Bob Ah. I see. You mean that blowing my brains out would be the reckless squandering of a valuable asset.
Mum Oh, you've always had a way of putting things just right, it's always a pleasure to hear you talk, pet.
Bob Thank you. Er—did you have any thoughts about it? Er— Dad?
Mum Oh, don't ask him, he's dead to the world that one.
Dad You should have married an ugly woman, son, like I did.

Mum goes into peals of merry laughter

Mum Hear that? Oh dear oh dear, they say he's senile but there's not much gets past him.

The lavatory flushes upstairs. Then the quack of the board

Dad I've had enough. (*He gets up*)
Mum We can't go yet, sit down.

Dad heads for the kitchen, as Shirley comes back in

Come back here, you!

Bob sits down, dispirited

Shirley You sit down, Mrs Hudd, I'll see he doesn't come to any harm, I'd point him in the right direction if he wants a little widdle.

Bob winces. Shirley starts to follow Dad. The doorbell rings

I'll get that, Bob, you rest those lovely little legs, that'll be Garry and Ronnie, if it's not my dreadful bloody husband.

Shirley goes

(*Off*) Garry! You sexy beast! Well, look at you! Yum yum yum! You get on in there, I'll attend to *you later*!
Bob (*more or less to himself*) This is a grown woman.

Gareth edges in rather uncertainly. A rather remarkable figure. He wears a hat with a feather in it, a tweed cape of the Sherlock Holmes variety, and plus twos. He is awkwardly carrying a very large picture wrapped up in red wrapping paper. Shirley follows him in and then goes out to the kitchen

Gareth Hello, Mother.
Mum Gareth! You shouldn't have!
Gareth Shouldn't have what? (*He seems a bit apprehensive*)
Mum Come all this way, just for us.
Gareth Oh, er—sorry.
Bob Sit down, Gareth. She doesn't mean it. It's just a thing people say.
Gareth Oh. Er, right. Right, yes. Fine. (*He sits, heavily. He takes his hat off and puts it in his lap. He has a bit of trouble leaning the picture*)
Mum And what have you got there, Gareth?
Gareth Oh, you know ... just a little something. To mark the occasion. Just, you know, something small. (*He tries to arrange it more conveniently and makes things worse*)

Dad marches out from the kitchen on his way to the stairs. He has a tin of nails in one hand and a big hammer in the other. He holds it as if he means business

Gareth glimpses him out of the corner of his eye and shies away. The picture falls

Oh, hello Dad.
Mum Sit down, you, and don't be ridiculous.

Thermal Underwear

Dad (*without stopping*) I'll get that bugger if it's the last thing I do.

Dad exits

Pause. We hear him stumping up the stairs

Gareth Well. Not every day you have your Ruby Wedding Anniversary.

The board quacks

Mum gets up and walks out purposefully after Dad

Did I say something? I mean, I wouldn't want to offend anyone. I've noticed lately ... hard to put this ... it's as if I sort of say something and people sort of look at me.

Bob I think a lot of us find that, Gareth. It's quite normal in conversations, I'm surprised you haven't noticed it before.

Gareth No, no, that's not quite what I meant, Bob. Ah ... how shall I put this? Er, funny looks.

Bob Ah. I see. I shouldn't worry about it. People can sometimes be taken aback by your originality, the way you crystallize the essential truth of a situation. "Not every day you have your Ruby Wedding Anniversary." "This is it," people think! "Gareth's gone straight to the heart of the matter!"

Gareth Oh. I see. Right. Fine. Mm. Well. Here we are then.

Bob looks at him

Yes! There! Like that!

Bob Yes, well, that was a perfect example of one of your crystallizations. Here we are then. *Yes.* (*He nods several times*)

Gareth Really. I'd have thought it was, well, a bit obvious myself. Still, when you come to think of it ... right. Yes. (*He nods a bit too*) Here we are.

Bob Gareth.

Gareth Yes, Bob?

Bob Do you ever experience a feeling of boredom so acute that it borders on homicidal rage?

Gareth Er, no. Don't think so, Bob. Very seldom bored. Life's full of interest.

Sudden loud banging: Dad nailing the board down. Whack, whack, whack, followed by a quack

Mum (*off*) Dad!
Gareth Good God what's that?
Bob I expect he's just giving it a few whacks.
Gareth Oh, I see. (*Pause*) Er, what? (*i.e. What's he whacking?*)

Whack, whack, whack, quack

Sounds like a duck.
Bob No, I don't think he's whacking a duck, Gareth.

Whack, whack, whack, quack

Mum (*off*) Dad! *Will* you leave that?

Whack, whack, whack

Elaine comes out from the kitchen

Elaine What the hell is he doing up there?

Whack, whack, whack, whack, whack. Pause. Quack

Bob Stubborn little creatures, these ducks.
Elaine For Christ's sake make him stop it!

Elaine goes back into the kitchen

Whack. Pause. Whack

Gareth No, you've got me wrong, Bob. I didn't actually think he was whacking a duck, I just thought it *sounded* like a duck.
Bob Ah, *I see*.

Whack, whack, whack

Gareth I expect he's just nailing down that loose board of yours.
Bob Oh, yes, that must be it.

Whack, whack. Pause. Quack

Gareth I saw a play about a duck once. I think it was a Norwegian duck. You know, Veronica dragged me along, she used to be all for that sort of thing.
Bob Ducks?
Gareth Plays. Bit too deep for me, I'm afraid. I didn't get a lot out of it.

Whack, whack, whack, whack, whack, whack, whack

Thermal Underwear

Elaine comes out from the kitchen

Elaine My God are you still sitting there, get up and stop him doing that!

Bob I think he must have nearly finished, darling.

Whack, whack, whack. Silence

Elaine (*staring at Bob balefully*) You bastard.

Bob smiles at her

Elaine turns and slams out to the kitchen again

Gareth Elaine's looking very fit.
Bob Thank you, Gareth. I try to keep her in trim.
Gareth Veronica's very fit too.
Bob Good.

Whack

A hammer would be an excellent thing to kill somebody else with, but it would be practically useless as a suicide weapon.
Gareth Er, yes. Right. Absolutely.
Bob In that respect it differs from a shotgun.
Gareth That's true. I never thought of it like that. (*Pleased*) That's a bit like one of my crystallizations, isn't it? (*A thought strikes him. He looks up anxiously*) You don't mean ... ?

Dad comes in, without the hammer, followed by Mum. Dad is breathing heavily from his efforts. They sit down on the sofa, both this time staring straight ahead

Dad That's a good job done.
Mum I'm not talking to him. He would not be told. Like a man possessed, he was. Look at him. Like a wild beast.
Dad Well it was grating on me.
Bob So you gave it a few whacks. Yes.

Shirley comes in from the kitchen carrying a tray with a champagne bottle and glasses

Shirley Here we are then! (*She puts the tray down. Stage whispering to Bob*) Elaine's in a bit of a state, Bob, what have you been doing to her, you sexy beast?
Bob Nothing, Shirley, nothing at all.

Shirley Well. That'll be it then, won't it? You need a bit of a tonic, you do. I'll have to take you down the lab and show you my rats. Anyway, get it open, let joy be unconfined eh?

Bob takes the bottle and starts to open it. (Orchestrate this properly in rehearsal: the wincing anticipations of the pop, etc.)

Elaine comes in fast with two plates of things on biscuits

Elaine Right then, we are *not* waiting any longer for Michael, we are *not* waiting any longer for Veronica, because *I* am ready for a *drink*, and if they can't be bothered to get here on time they can stuff themselves! We have caviare and cream cheese, we have smoked salmon and cream cheese, and for those who don't like caviare and smoked salmon, we have——

Bob Cream cheese?

Elaine (*savagely*) Right, and for those who don't like cream cheese we have *dry biscuits*, all right, darling?

Mum Dad and I don't like caviare and smoked salmon, Elaine, you know that.

Elaine Oh, *fine*!

Dad I like anything that's good to eat.

Mum No he doesn't. Give him the cream cheese.

People are taking things off the plates. Bob is still wrestling with the bottle

Elaine Oh, for God's sake, Bob, what's the matter with you?

Bob (*more or less to himself*) Mid-life crisis, general debility, piles, dandruff, melancholia, terminal boredom, paranoia . . .

Shirley Isn't it funny, Mick's the only one of us who really likes caviare, and he's not here!

Bob Yes. It's bloody hilarious, that. Nearly there.

Everyone is wincing except Dad. Now Bob can be as long as it takes for the cork to pop. If it takes a long time Elaine can put in a "Oh for God's sake Bob!". The cork comes out

Mum Ooh!
Gareth Hooray!
Dad What the hell was that?
Elaine Brilliant, darling.
Bob (*pouring*) Thank you.

Mum Small one for him. We don't want him, you know.
Bob (*handing the glasses*) Mother-in-law. Dad. Help yourselves.
Shirley Well. The happy couple! Mr and Mrs Hudd!
Gareth Mum and Dad, forty years together!
Dad I'll drink to that. (*He does. A big swig*)
Mum You're not *supposed* to drink to that! *They're* supposed to drink to *that*!
Dad I like a drink: Absent friends!
Gareth Absent friends!

Dad drains his glass and holds it out. Bob refills it

Mum Don't give him any more, you know what he's like
Bob It's his special day. It's *your* special day.
Mum Oh, one day's very much like the next when you get to our age, you know, Bob.
Elaine Oh, great, so we needn't have bothered with all this, that's wonderful.
Mum Not on our account, Elaine.
Elaine Oh, *splendid*! That *is* good news. (*Turning on Gareth, just because he's there*) So why couldn't your *wife* be bothered to make it?
Gareth Well, I'm not quite sure, Elaine. Gather she's got something on. You know.
Elaine *What sort of thing?*
Gareth Oh, you know, Elaine. One of her things.
Shirley Like Mick.
Gareth Yes, I suppose so. In point of fact I think it's *with* Mick. She's got some sort of thing on the go with Mick, seems to keep her quite busy.
Elaine *What sort of thing?*
Gareth Well, I don't like to stick my nose in, Elaine. Veronica's a bit fed up with me these days, you know. I expect she finds Mick a bit more stimulating to talk to.
Mum That's it. Well Mick's got a bit of life about him. Mick knows how to put the cat among the pigeons. Oh, dear. (*She chuckles happily*)

Elaine is transfixed

Shirley I expect they're just having a bit of fling, Gareth. I shouldn't worry too much. Mick never sticks at anything for long. He's very lively, my husband, but he lacks staying power.

Gareth Yes, well, didn't like to stick my nose in. She seems to get annoyed with me very easily these days.

Dad is steadily eating his way through all this

Elaine God, Gareth! Are you alive? Is anything actually going on in there?

Gareth Well. Um ... have to come back to you on that one, Elaine.

Mum You're keeping warm though, aren't you, Gareth?

Gareth Oh, yes Mum, no problems there.

Mum That's it. Ever since I got into that thermal underwear, I've been able to let the rest of the world go by.

Shirley Well, this is it, Mrs Hudd.

Elaine stares at them in disbelief. She picks up the champagne bottle, changes her mind, goes upstage and pours herself a stiff vodka instead. She hugs it to her, taking sips from it

Bob Actually, there's something I've been meaning to ask you for a while, Gareth.

Gareth What's that, then, Bob?

Bob Well, it's a bit personal.

Gareth Fire away.

Bob Why do you wear such bloody silly clothes?

Gareth I'm glad you asked me that, Bob. Bit of a tricky one. Um ... let's see. How to put it. Well, er ... after the rationalization at Masters and Kellett ...

Bob When they gave you the sack, yes.

Gareth Well, that's not strictly accurate, Bob, it was more in the nature of an involuntary early retirement ...

Mum Booted him out after all those years, wasn't it a disgrace?

Gareth And well, what with Veronica getting a bit sort of fed up with me ...

Shirley ... going out with all and sundry, well you can't blame her ...

Gareth I thought the thing might be to try and make myself a bit more interesting.

Bob I see, Gareth. Thank you. How d'you think it's working out?

Thermal Underwear

Gareth Not sure, in point of fact. Think it might be a bit of a long-term project.
Shirley Well I think you look lovely, Gareth, with your socks and your little legs and everything.
Gareth (*pleased*) Thank you, Shirley. (*Wanting to reciprocate*) Er, how are the rats?
Elaine Oh, Christ, not the rats. This is the worst day of my life.
Mum Don't you take any notice of her, Shirley. You tell us about your rats if you want to, pet.
Shirley Well, actually, we've had quite a little breakthrough at the lab, everyone's very excited.

Elaine fumes, drinks, and then pours another

Bob Including the rats?
Shirley Especially the rats, Bob. You see Dr Northcott's worked out how to wire up electrodes to the pleasure centres in their brains.
Elaine Oh, God.
Shirley It's very interesting, Elaine, I should have thought you'd be fascinated, you see what that means is that we can give them their little orgasms just by pressing a button.
Bob That's wonderful, Shirley. You mean they don't have to take each other out to dinner and discuss the meaning of their relationship and whether it's really fair on old Thingumyjig or whatever these things are like in the rat world ...
Shirley Exactly. Press a button ... and the earth moves for them.
Elaine Shirley d'you really feel that this is the right context for a lecture on rats' climaxes?
Shirley Oh, Mr and Mrs Hudd don't mind, do you Mr and Mrs Hudd, I expect you've had more climaxes in your time than we've had hot dinners, haven't you?
Dad I wouldn't mind a hot dinner now.
Mum Shut up you. Go on, Shirley, we're all ears.
Shirley Well, then 'it was weeks and weeks training them to understand which button to press. They all knew already how to get their food and their water, but Dr Northcott said it was very important they knew what they were choosing. Well anyway, I won't bore you with the details, the thing is, when they knew which button was which, they pressed the orgasm button every

time, isn't that amazing? Sixteen times a minute, some of them, twenty-four hours a day!

Bob Yes. Ah, Shirley, do let me know if Dr Northcott perfects his little device for human use. Might just solve that Christmas present problem.

Elaine You bastard.

Gareth Er, what happened to the rats, Shirley? Were they all right, sort of thing?

Shirley No, of course they weren't all right, Gareth, how d'you think you'd stand up to it? Most of them were gone with heart attacks in the first two days, poor little things, but there were a few really tough ones kept going for a week, till they starved to death. It's funny, how involved you'd get, sort of willing them on ... I thought they were—sort of heroic, in a way. Anyway—it makes you think, doesn't it?

Elaine (*trembling, in quite a state*) Shirley. Rats are—rats are not like human beings. Human beings have—human beings have dignity!

Shirley You reckon?

Pause

Gareth Er—Mum, Dad ... Veronica and I got you a little something, just to mark the occasion ... er, is it all right if I give it to them now, Elaine?

Elaine You can do what you bloody well like, Gareth.

Gareth Er, right. Fine, well, it's just a little thing, really ... (*He struggles with the huge painting*)

Mum Oh, you shouldn't have. There wasn't any need. You know we don't like a fuss.

Gareth (*pulling the wrapping paper off*) Just thought it might ... well, in point of fact I'm very chuffed with myself for thinking of it ...

We can see it now. A large Canaletto reproduction

Mum Is it a picture, Gareth?

Gareth That's right, Mum. (*He turns it round proudly so that she can see it*) Thought it might bring back happy memories.

Mum Oh. What of, Gareth?

Gareth Well. You know, *Venice*.

Thermal Underwear

Mum But we ... oh, dear, oh dear. Never mind, love, it was a lovely thought.

Dad starts speaking as if someone's pressed a button

Dad I remember that holiday as if it was yesterday. Grand Canal. By, that was a sight. Ay, but most of all that boat trip to Murano. All right on the way *out* there. All right *there*. The heat in that glassblowing place. Watching the glass-blowers. That was artistry. The colours, the way the light came through the reds and the greens, hold your hand up, see little pools of red and green light on your skin ... and the heat of it. We couldn't afford much then, but we just had to have one of those little red bowls with the gold on it; the way that girl wrapped it up, that was an art in itself. And then coming back. Squall blew up from nowhere. The sky was black. And in no time at all the water was coming over the sides and up through the boards and I said to your mother she's going over, you know, and she said don't be silly, John, and then this bloody big black wave came and over we went ... I never left go of your mother, I could see some of them getting swept away, but I had one arm round her, and one holding on to the keel. But I had to let that parcel go. John, John, she said, don't let our little bowl go, but I said, I know what's more precious than that, and I held her there like that, one arm round her, the other hand holding the keel, till the rescue boat came. Ay. You don't forget that sort of thing in a hurry.

Pause

Mum I might have known we'd get that one. Oh, dear, oh dear. How many times d'you think you've told them that story?
Shirley I think it's a lovely story, Mrs Hudd.

A drop of water falls on Dad's head. He puts his hand up, stares around

Dad Hey, what's this?
Mum But you don't understand, Shirley ...
Dad Me head's all wet.
Mum Oh, don't be so stupid, how can your head be wet?

Another big drop falls

Dad There's water falling on me head.
Mum Don't take any notice of him, you're *inside*, you don't get wet in the *house*.
Shirley (*feeling*) His head is wet.
Mum Well how's he gone and got his head wet?
Elaine Oh, my God, I'll tell you how he's got his head wet, he's gone and banged a nail through the water pipe! (*Standing over her father and yelling at him*) You stupid old man, you've banged a nail through the water pipe!

Dad is staring straight ahead. He begins to tremble

(*Turning on Bob*) Do something!
Bob (*to Mum*) Is he all right?
Mum He's just having one of his turns, Bob.
Elaine You stupid, senile old vandal!
Mum It's no good, Elaine, he can't hear you. Hey, I think it's dripping on me as well, oh dear, oh dear.
Elaine (*to Bob*) Get up there and *do* something!
Bob Elaine, I hardly think a few more drops of water are going to make much difference to him now.
Elaine I'm not talking about *him*, I'm talking about the ceiling, d'you want it all down on our heads or what?
Bob To be quite frank with you, Elaine, I don't actually give a fart one way or the other.

Elaine glares at Bob for a second

Elaine Gareth, Shirley, come up with me, we've got to do something!

Elaine rushes off

Gareth and Shirley look at each other

Gareth Er, better, I s'pose.
Shirley She's in ever such a state today.

Gareth and Shirley look at each other

Mum (*almost proudly*) Look at him. Dead to the world. You'd never think he could cause that much trouble, would you?
Elaine (*off*) Well don't just stand there, Gareth! We've got to get that board up!

Thermal Underwear

Gareth (*off*) Er, don't you think it would be better to——
Elaine (*off*) Oh, shut up and just bloody do it, will you?
Mum It's funny how he always tells that story. The thing was, we never went to Venice.
Bob What?
Mum No, Bob, the firm went bust just before we were due to go. We got our money back. Bought our bedroom carpet with it. But all that boat trip business, I don't know where that came from. The human mind's a funny thing, don't you think, Bob?
Elaine (*off*) Oh, come *on*, Gareth!

We hear the board come up with a great groaning quack. Elaine screams

(*Off*) Bob! Help! Bob!

Bob smiles

(*Off*) Bob!
Mum (*getting up*) I'd better go and see what's going on, you keep an eye on that one, Bob.

Elaine keeps yelling upstairs

Elaine (*off*) Shirley! Get your finger on that! Christ! Bob!
Mum (*off*) Oh, dear, oh dear.
Bob (*to Dad*) I'd really like to know the secret. I'd really like to know how to (*pause**) shut it all out, you know? I sincerely admire the way you manage all that. D'you think I've got a chance of getting there? I don't mean straightaway, of course, but if I thought there was a good chance that one day I'd be able to view the world with that (*pause**) totally disinterested serenity ... well, it would be quite a comfort.

Gareth rushes in

Gareth Stopcock! Where?
Bob Kitchen, Gareth. Behind the door.
Gareth Er, right. Fine.

Gareth goes out to the kitchen

Bob (*to Dad*) Rather like thermal underwear.

Mum comes in, quite excited

Mum Oh dear, oh dear, you should go up and have a look, Bob, it's like Trafalgar Square up there, all these little jets of water going everywhere! He must have gone through that pipe in ten places! And our Elaine flat on her face trying to jam 'em up with her fingers, oh dear, oh dear! (*To Dad*) Oh, you've done it this time. Eh, what a shame Mick couldn't come, he does like a laugh and fair do's he's very handy in a crisis.
Bob Er, d'you think he looks a bit blue?
Mum No, love, it's just one of his turns. Look at him, caused all this bother and there he sits, dead to the world!

Gareth emerges from the kitchen

Gareth Turned the water off. Ought to go down now. Er, is Dad all right? Doesn't he look a bit sort of blue?
Mum Oh, he's right as rain, that one, never better, he can turn that on at will, sometimes I think it's just to gain the sympathy.

Elaine comes in, dripping wet. Her hairstyle destroyed, wet hair plastered down

Mum Eh, look at our Elaine! Eh, you're like a drowned rat!

Shirley follows Elaine in. Shirley is less wet

Elaine (*trembling, going to Dad*) You stupid, stubborn, foolish old man! This is the last, the very last time you come to this house! I just can't... I just can't... (*She is more or less crying with rage*)
Mum (*cheerfully*) It's no use love, he can't hear you, dead to the world, this one!
Shirley Is he, is he all right? He looks a bit blue.
Elaine He's all right! He's just bloody well pretending, like he's always done! You heard me all right! Didn't you? Didn't you?
Gareth Elaine. (*He is uncharacteristically strong here*) Leave him alone.

Elaine turns. During the following, Shirley goes over to Dad and feels for a pulse

Elaine Oh, God. I'm sorry. I don't like being like this, I don't like myself like this. It's not him at all, it's not him, I know he can't help it, it's... what it really is is how you get when you live with someone like Bob. And there's nothing there, you see, you think he's alive, he moves he speaks, but there isn't, there isn't

Thermal Underwear

anything, it's like living... it's like living with a block of frozen shit.

Shirley (*mouthing to Gareth*) I think he's dead.

Mum (*cheerfully*) Well, I daresay it'll all come out in the wash, Elaine. Now I've been looking at that parcel all afternoon, would that be a little something for us as well?

Elaine (*subdued*) Yes it would, Mum.

Mum Eh, you shouldn't have bothered.

Elaine No, I don't suppose I should have. It's a Teasmade.

Mum But we've got a Teasmade.

Elaine It's a new model. It's better, it's improved, I thought you'd like the new one, well, I couldn't think of anything you'd want.

Mum Well, that's right, Elaine, you don't when you get to our age. No, pet, it was a lovely thought, but we're quite happy with the old one, it'll see us through nicely, pet. No, I'll tell you what, you and Bob keep this one, we'd like you to have it, wouldn't we, Dad? (*She looks at him properly for the first time*) Dad?

It's an agonizing moment

Dad No, we'll have the new one. Let them have the old one. Whose bloody anniversary is it?

Pause as they stare at him

Have I had my tea yet?

Elaine You old...! We thought you were...!

Shirley Is he all right?

Mum Course he's all right, just one of his little goes, wasn't it, Dad? Think we'd better be getting you home now. Done enough for one day, eh?

Dad Gave it a few whacks.

Elaine Oh, *God*!

Dad (*thoughtfully*) It's not that hard, you know, when you get a bit of practice in.

Dad turns to Bob who has been looking at him with deep respect

I dare say you'll get the hang of it, Bob. I dare say you'll all get the hang of it. As the years go by.

They stare at him

Dad exits slowly as——

··· the Lights fade gradually to Black-out

FURNITURE AND PROPERTY LIST

On stage: Hi-fi cabinet. *On it:* phone
Stool
Table. *On it:* tray of drinks (including vodka) and glasses
Sofa. *On it:* Elaine's handbag containing diary etc.
Coffee-table. *On it:* bulky parcel in wrapping paper

Off stage: Large Canaletto reproduction wrapped in red gift paper **(Gareth)**
Tin of nails, large hammer **(Dad)**
Tray, unopened bottle of champagne, 6 glasses **(Shirley)**
2 plates containing smoked salmon, cream cheese, caviare etc. on biscuits **(Elaine)**

LIGHTING PLOT

Property fittings required: nil

Interior. The same scene throughout

To open: Full general lighting

Cue 1 **Dad** exits slowly (Page 23)
Fade gradually to Black-out

EFFECTS PLOT

Cue 1	**Elaine** (*singing*): "Every move you make ..." *Floorboard noise*	(Page 1)
Cue 2	**Elaine** puts the phone down *Car draws up*	(Page 2)
Cue 3	**Elaine** makes for the door fast *Car doors slam, front door opens and closes*	(Page 2)
Cue 4	**Mum:** "Talk to yourself." *Floorboard noise*	(Page 3)
Cue 5	**Mum:** "Girls not here, Bob?" *Floorboard noise*	(Page 3)
Cue 6	**Mum:** "... will of her own, that one." *Floorboard noise*	(Page 4)
Cue 7	**Elaine** (*off, from above*): "Ready!" *Floorboard noise*	(Page 5)
Cue 8	**Bob:** "... a bit of advice." *Doorbell*	(Page 6)
Cue 9	**Mum:** "... isn't it, Dad?" *Floorboard noise*	(Page 8)
Cue 10	**Mum:** "... not much gets past him." *Lavatory flush, floorboard noise*	(Page 9)
Cue 11	**Shirley** starts to follow Dad *Doorbell*	(Page 10)
Cue 12	**Dad** exits *Pause, then footsteps stumping up the stairs*	(Page 11)
Cue 13	**Gareth:** "... your Ruby Wedding Anniversary" *Floorboard noise*	(Page 11)
Cue 14	**Gareth:** "Life's full of interest." *Loud banging and floorboard noises as pages 11–13*	(Page 11)
Cue 15	**Shirley:** "... a lovely story, Mrs Hudd." *Water begins to drip from above*	(Page 19)
Cue 16	**Elaine** (*off*): "Oh, come *on*, Gareth!" *Great groaning noise of floorboard*	(Page 21)
Cue 17	**Gareth** emerges from the kitchen *Gradually stop water drip*	(Page 22)

www.ingramcontent.com/pod-product-compliance
Lightning Source LLC
Chambersburg PA
CBHW070455050426
42450CB00012B/3289